L•LEONARD
STRUMENTAL
PLAY-ALONG

D0503926

ALTO SAX

AUDIO
ACCESS
INCLUDED

PLAYBACK+
ed • Pitch • Balance • Loop

Movie and TV Music

The Avengers 2
Captain America March 3
Doctor Who XI 4
Downton Abbey 5
Game of Thrones 6
Guardians of the Galaxy 7
Hawaii Five-O Theme 8
Married Life (from *UP*) 9
Outlander Theme (The Skye Boat Song) 10
Prologue and Prologue Part 2 (from *Beauty and the Beast*) 11
Rey's Theme (from *Star Wars: The Force Awakens*) 12
Test Drive (from *How to Train Your Dragon*) 16
Theme from The X-Files 14

Audio Arrangements by Peter Deneff

To access audio visit:
www.halleonard.com/mylibrary
Enter Code
8702-9206-8867-5648

ISBN 978-1-5400-2064-2

HAL•LEONARD®

Visit Hal Leonard Online at
www.halleonard.com

Contact Us:
Hal Leonard
7777 West Bluemound Road
Milwaukee, WI 53213
Email: info@halleonard.com

In Europe contact:
Hal Leonard Europe Limited
Distribution Centre, Newmarket Road
Bury St Edmunds, Suffolk, IP33 3YB
Email: info@halleonardeurope.com

In Australia contact:
Hal Leonard Australia Pty. Ltd.
4 Lentara Court
Cheltenham, Victoria, 3192 Australia
Email: info@halleonard.com.au

THE AVENGERS

from THE AVENGERS

ALTO SAX

Composed by
ALAN SILVESTRI

CAPTAIN AMERICA MARCH

from CAPTAIN AMERICA

ALTO SAX

By ALAN SILVESTRI

DOCTOR WHO XI

ALTO SAX

By MURRAY GOLD

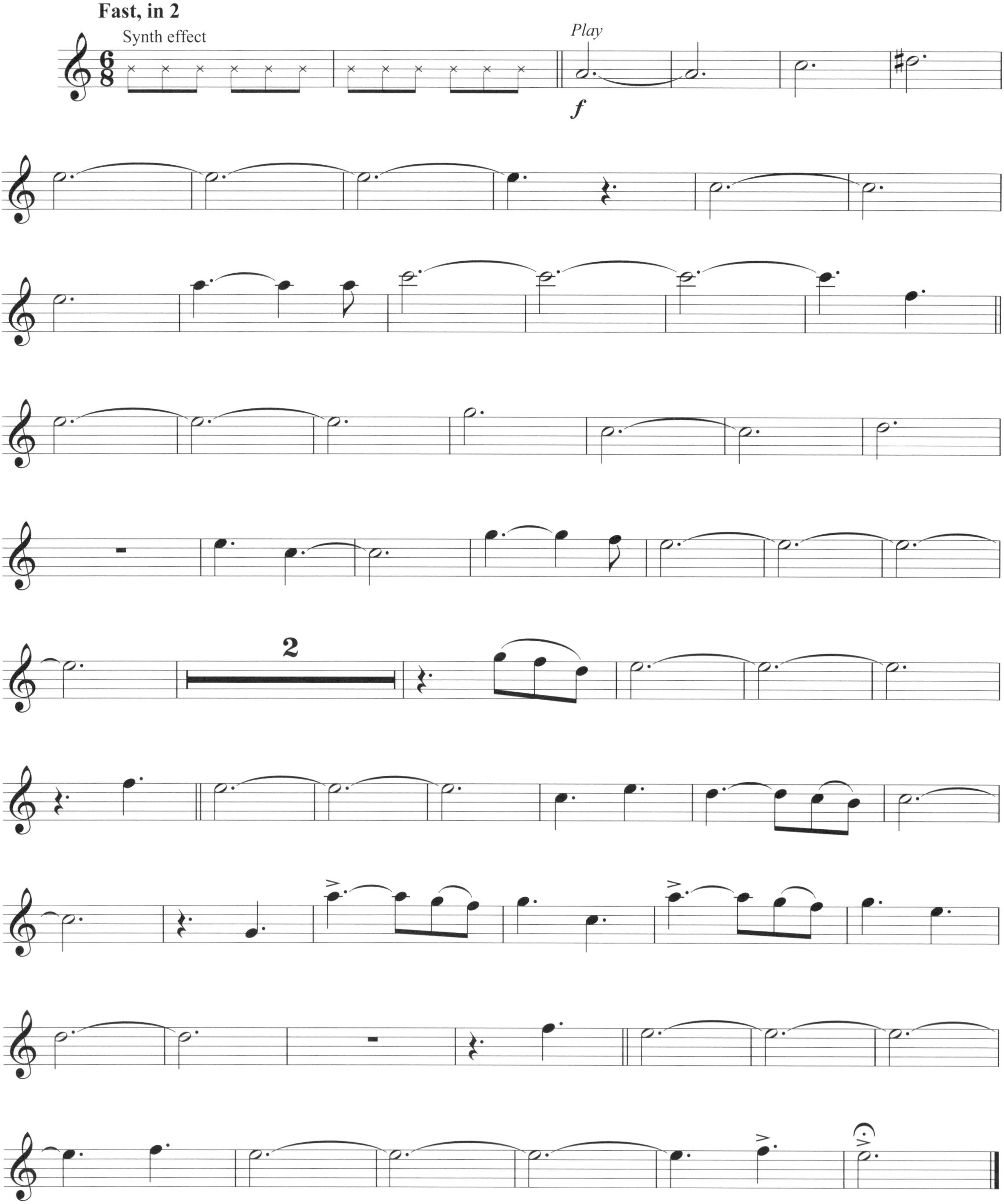

DOWNTON ABBEY
(Theme)

ALTO SAX

Music by JOHN LUNN

GAME OF THRONES

Theme from the HBO Series GAME OF THRONES

ALTO SAX

By RAMIN DJAWADI

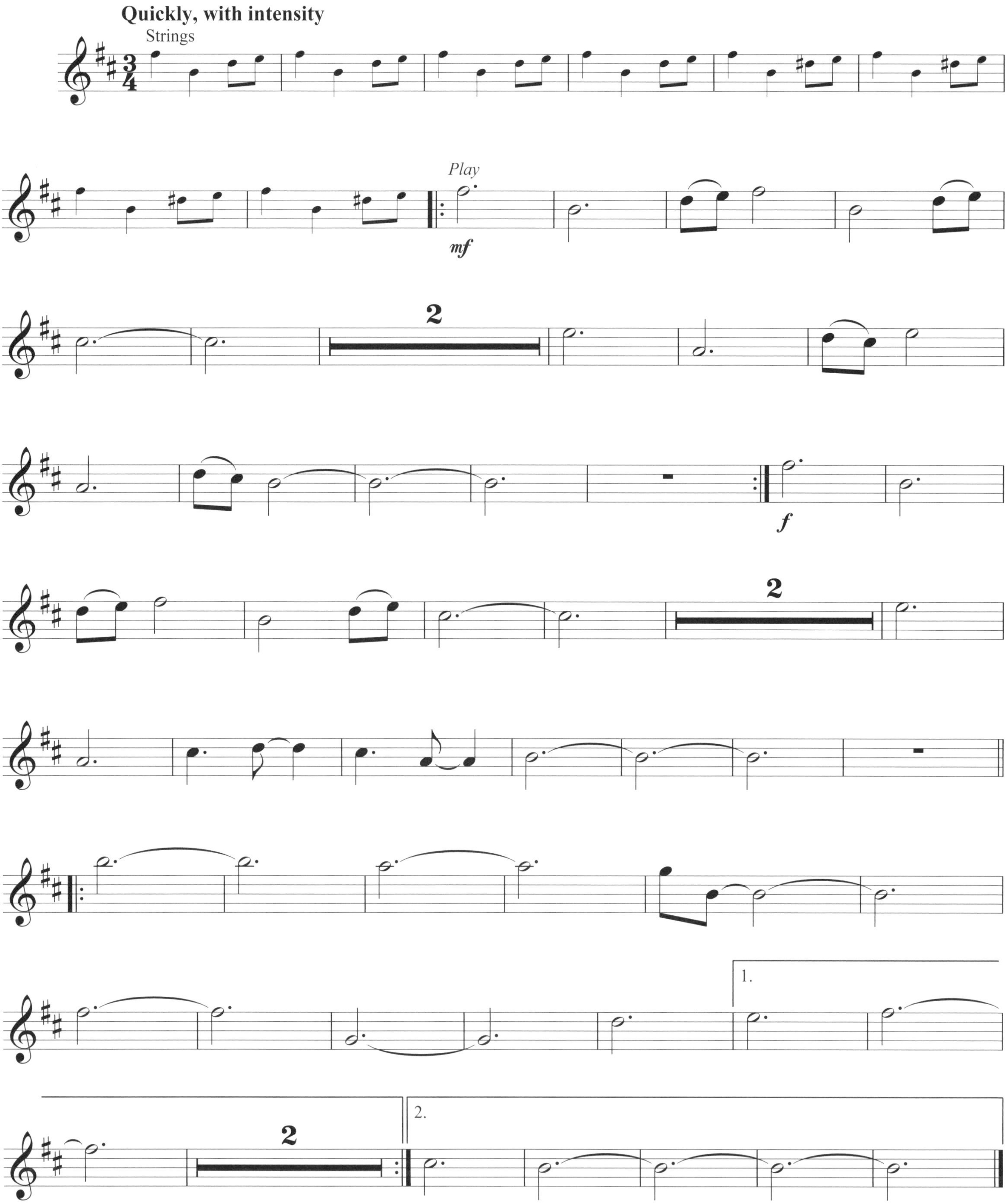

GUARDIANS OF THE GALAXY

from GUARDIANS OF THE GALAXY

ALTO SAX

Composed by TYLER BATES,
DIETER HARTMANN, TIMOTHY WILLIAMS
and KURT OLDMAN

HAWAII FIVE-O THEME

from the Television Series

ALTO SAX

By MORT STEVENS

MARRIED LIFE

from UP

ALTO SAX

By MICHAEL GIACCHINO

OUTLANDER THEME
(The Skye Boat Song)

ALTO SAX

Traditional Music
Arranged by BEAR McCREARY

PROLOGUE AND PROLOGUE PART 2

from BEAUTY AND THE BEAST

ALTO SAX

PROLOGUE
Music by ALAN MENKEN

Moderately

PROLOGUE PART 2
Music by ALAN MENKEN and CHRISTOPHER BENSTEAD

REY'S THEME
from STAR WARS: THE FORCE AWAKENS

ALTO SAX

Music by JOHN WILLIAMS

mf
Broadly
f
ff
rit.
Tempo I
mp
p
rit.
pp

THEME FROM THE X-FILES

from the Twentieth Century Fox Television Series THE X-FILES

ALTO SAX

By MARK SNOW

mp
mf
mp
p

TEST DRIVE

from the Motion Picture HOW TO TRAIN YOUR DRAGON

ALTO SAX

By JOHN POWELL